ELEMENTS OF THE **EXTRAORDINARY**

Handwriting Analysis

Can you read your character?

ELEMENTS OF THE **EXTRAORDINARY**

Handwriting Analysis

Can you read your character?

JACQUI TEW

ELEMENT
CHILDREN'S BOOKS

SHAFTESBURY, DORSET · BOSTON, MASSACHUSETTS · MELBOURNE, VICTORIA

© Element Children's Books 1998
Text © Jacqui Tew 1998

First published in Great Britain in 1998 by
Element Children's Books, Shaftesbury, Dorset SP7 8BP

Published in the USA in 1998 by Element Books Inc.
160 North Washington Street, Boston, MA 02114

Published in Australia in 1998 by
Element Books Limited and distributed by Penguin Books Australia Ltd,
487 Maroondah Highway, Ringwood, Victoria 3134

Reprinted 1998

Cover design by Ness Wood
Cover photography credits: PEN, HAND AND PEN
– by courtesy of Jon Stone

Typeset by Dorchester Typesetting Group Ltd
Printed and bound in Great Britain by Creative Print and Design

British Library Cataloguing in Publication data available.
Library of Congress Cataloging in Publication data available.

ISBN 1 901881 30 X

TO MY PARENTS
For their patience, help, support and encouragement

Acknowledgements

I would particularly like to thank my mother for the enormous amount of time and energy she has given to helping in all the aspects of writing a book. Special thanks also to Angela Lorimer and Maureen Butterfield for their patient, loving support and encouragement, and thanks also to Bridget Thomas.

My thanks to the following children who kindly gave me their handwriting for use in the book: Peter Bentley; Alice Bush; Catherine Long; Hayley Long; Jessica Lorimer; Mark McDonnell; Rachel Percival; and James Snider.

My thanks also to the following schools for their help in producing samples of writing: Bohunt and Highfield (both in Liphook); St Andrew's (Nuthurst); Cleves (Oatlands); Danesfield Preparatory (Walton); Staines Preparatory; The American Community School (Cobham); The Dawney (Great Bookham); and St Charles, Heathside, St James, and St Maur's (all in Weybridge).

AUTHOR'S NOTE

The author has made every effort to maintain the anonymity of all those persons whose handwriting samples appear in the book. The interpretations accompanying each sample represent the author's analysis, based on generally accepted graphological principles, and make no comment on the character of any particular individual.

Contents

Glossary

Baseline   The imaginary line upon which you write.

Baseline (concave)   The baseline dips in the middle of the line and then rises at the finish.

Baseline (convex)   The baseline rises in the middle of the line and then falls at the finish.

Baseline (falling)   The baseline falls across the page.

Baseline (rising)   The baseline rises across the page.

Baseline (straight)   The baseline runs straight across the page.

Baseline (wavy)   The baseline goes up and down across the page.

Connected   Most or all of the letters in each word are joined up.

Disconnected   All or most of the letters in each word are not joined up.

Flowery   See style.

Line spacing (close or narrow) The lines on the page are close but not touching.

Line spacing (mingling) The movements in the lower zone touch the movements in the upper zone on the next line.

Line spacing (wide) There is plenty of space between each line.

Pressure The mark or indentation that is made with the pen through the paper.

Regularity (irregular) The writing is different in size, zones, spacing, and maybe slant.

Regularity (regular) The writing looks the same in size, zones, spacing, and slant.

Rhythm (arrhythm) There is no flow to the writing. It looks disjointed or jerky.

Rhythm (flow) The flow of the writing (think of a river flowing along) will have the same sort of ripples as a river, and look pleasing to your eye.

Signature The way people sign their names is how they see themselves. When this is different from the way they write normally, they will see themselves differently from the way their friends see them.

Simplified See style.

Size (large) The whole size measures more than 12mm ($^{1}/_{2}$in). Discerning the whole size entails measuring from the tops of the letters "b", "d", "f", "h", "k", "l", and "t" to the bottoms of the letters "f", "g", "j", "q", and "y".

Size (medium) The whole size measures between 9-12mm ($^{3}/_{8}$ and $^{1}/_{2}$in).

Size (small) The whole size measure less than 9mm ($^{3}/_{8}$in).

Slant (left) The writing slopes backwards.

Slant (mixed)   The slope of the writing slants sometimes to the right and sometimes to the left.

Slant (right)   The writing slopes forwards.

Slant (upright)   The writing stands up straight without sloping to left or right.

Spacing   See line and word spacing.

Stroke (fine or thin)   A thin or fine pen has been used.

Stroke (thick)   A wide or thick stroke is produced on the paper from the chosen pen of the writer.

Style   What we choose to do and how we have changed our writing from the copybook style we were taught.

Style (flowery)   Extra curls and loops are added to the writing.

Style (simplified)   The writing only has the basic movements.

Word spacing (close or narrow)   The words are closely spaced together. The letter "n" of the writer will not fit into the space between each word.

Word spacing (normal)   The letter "n" of the writer fits into the space between each word.

Word spacing (wide)   More than one letter "n" from the writer will fit into the space between each word.

Width (broad or wide)   The space between the two strokes that form the letter "n" is larger on the baseline than the height of the strokes.

Width (narrow)   The space between the two strokes that form the letter "n" is narrower on the baseline than the height of the strokes.

Width (normal)   The letter is square. The space between the two strokes that form the letter "n" is the same size as the height of each stroke.

Zone (lower)   The descenders (lower stems) in the following letters: "f", "g", "j", "p", "q", "y", and sometimes "z".

Zone (middle)   This is found in the following letters: "a", "c", "e", "i", "m", "n", "o", "r", "s", "u", "v", "w", "x", and sometimes "z".

Zone (upper)   The ascenders (upper stems) in the following letters: "b", "d", "f", "h", "k", "l", and "t".

Introduction

Before you read any further, write a sample of your handwriting spontaneously (in other words, write whatever comes into your head) on unlined paper so you can study it later.

What is the Reason for Writing?

Each time you put pen to paper you are trying to send a message – whether it is a list to remind you of the things you need to do or writing to tell a friend your news. All forms of writing transmit information of some sort.

Graphology, the study of handwriting, has been developed over many hundreds of years as a way to discover people's characters. Gradually a set of rules was created about the meaning of each handwriting movement (the name we give to each separate element of handwriting, such as the formation of each letter). These rules are so wide-ranging and are taken so seriously that, today, anyone wanting a career as a graphologist has to study for three years.

Q. Is graphology a science or an art?

A. It is both. Set rules are followed to break down the writing into specific parts and a scientific approach is used for precise measurements. It is an art because in order to arrive at a final and accurate description of the personality, we have to synthesise all the findings into a cohesive whole.

Writing shows how we express our feelings, so it stands to reason that the Italians write in a much more lively and spontaneous way than the British because they are known for showing their feelings instantly. However, we cannot always tell which country a person comes from by looking at his or her writing.

How Graphology Works

To find the right character interpretation we have to approach the analysis scientifically. This means taking careful measurements in order to assess the handwriting movements correctly – you cannot do this by guesswork. Your artistic skills are used when deciding which explanation of each movement is the most accurate description of the person concerned.

As the first graphology students in Germany discovered, it is VERY important to identify at least three different movements in a piece of writing that indicate a particular personality trait. You should never assess someone's character on the basis of only one handwriting movement. For instance, if a person is ambitious, then his or her writing may have heavy pressure, rising baselines and large size – three indications of ambition. There are other movements that also indicate when someone is keen to succeed, and you will learn more about these as you read this book.

When we put pen to paper we make a unique and individual pattern. Some of the movements that we make happen all the time, but others do not. You can test this for yourself – if you write your signature six times you will see that although it may look more or less the same each time, there are little differences too. When studying graphology we are particularly interested in the writing movements that happen all the time. Some of these dominant movements are the size, slant, flow, and width of the writing. We will talk more about these in the rest of the book.

CHAPTER 1

Origins and History

No one knows when handwriting was first analyzed, but we do know that Aristotle, the philosopher who lived from 384-322 BC, wrote: "Just as all men do not have the same speech sounds, neither do they all have the same writing." We also know that the Roman Emperor Augustus had his writing analyzed. He died in AD 14, so the idea of handwriting analysis has existed for at least 2,000 years.

It was not until the 12th and 13th centuries that people in general began to learn how to write. Until then, they used professional writers called scribes. The first book on graphology was published in 1621 by Camillo Baldi, an Italian.

However, serious research into graphology did not begin until the 19th century, when a group of French monks began a study of many hundreds of different handwritings. The man in charge was a priest called Michon, and he became known as the grandfather of graphology. In 1871 he invented the word "graphology" from two Greek words: "graph," meaning "writing," and "ology" which is the suffix (something added to the end of a word) to anything that is scientifically studied.

Michon set up rules for interpretation. His theory was that each writing movement had a particular meaning. For instance, he said that large writing indicates ambition and a right slant means the writer is emotional. His interpretations worked most of the time but he wasn't always right.

Some German students heard about Michon and traveled to France to learn from him. After much study they decided that, in order to be correct all the time, it was important to find three different writing movements that all indicated the same meaning. Looking at the sample below, one of the characteristics of this writer is that she is a hard worker. This shows in three ways: most of the letters within each word are joined up; heavy pressure; and slightly wide word spacing.

> lots of people to enjc
> adventure, and even t
> ement that females
> can do it for the
> Geri was born
> 6th August 1972, with
> and a Spanish mum
> Geri is an a

Today, Germans are world leaders. Anyone applying for a job in Germany knows that his or her handwriting will be analyzed as a matter of course. It doesn't matter if you are applying to do something practical like gardening or carpentry, or whether you are going to be a company director. Every job applicant submits his or her handwriting without thinking twice about it. Could that be a reason for Germany's success in industry and business?

Fascinating Facts

There are certain facts that even graphologists cannot tell from studying someone's handwriting. Look at the writing below and see if you can guess:

◆✦ The age of the writer.

◆✦ If it is a man or a woman.

"I have a kitten, my dearest
drollest of all creatures that
Skin. Here gambols are not t
would be incredible, if they c

When I was given this sample of writing I had no idea of the writer's age or sex, and was totally wrong with both my guesses!

Turn to the Answers section at the back of the book to see if you have guessed correctly.

Q. I have heard about foot and mouth artists who are unable to use their hands. Can you analyze their writing?

A. Yes. Every time you write, whether it is with your hand, your mouth, or even your foot, a message starts out from your brain and then travels along your nerves and muscles until it reaches where the pen is being held. (See Chapter 20.)

Q. Why is my writing sometimes different?

A. Your writing changes according to the way you feel. When you are tired your writing will alter to show the tiredness and when you are excited your writing will be much more lively. However, your writing will basically stay the same, it is only the little things that will change.

Q. Was writing always the same in the past?

A. No. Writing was straight up and down, with no slant, until the middle of the 16th century. It was at the time of Queen Elizabeth I that a right slant was first noticed.

A man called Robert Saudek, who was a very famous graphologist, collected handwritings for many years. He studied the writings of some men who had been blinded in battle and discovered that they were still writing in exactly the same way as they did when they could see. Although they could no longer see, they still had the same personality and it is this that is expressed in handwriting.

Another famous handwriting analyst called Hans Jacoby discovered that people's writing can change when they are hypnotized into believing they are someone else. Why do you think this is?

How Do I Start?

There are five steps to take when analyzing writing:

1 First you will need some handwriting to analyze! When asking someone for his or her writing you will also have to find out some information about him or her (see below).

2 You can then make a note of his or her writing movements.

3 Next, look up the interpretations for each movement and write them down.

4 Check with the A-Z section at the back of the book to make sure your interpretations for each personality characteristic are correct.

5 Write a few notes or have a chat with the person whose writing you have just analyzed and tell him or her your findings.

What to Ask Before Analyzing Someone's Writing

Let's look at the questions you need to ask someone before studying his or her writing, and why these are important:

◆◆ The age of the writer. This is impossible to guess and if you do not know it you could make an embarrassing mistake.

◆◆ Is the writer male or female? This is an easy question to answer when your friends want their writing analyzed, but could be difficult if a stranger writes to you and signs his or her name Chris or Pat. This could mean Christopher or Christine, Patricia or Patrick. It is not possible to tell the sex of a person from his or her writing so, if in doubt, ask!

◆◆ The nationality of the person and the country in which he or she learned to write. If you are American and learned to write in England, you will have been taught to write in a different way to that of your friends who learned to write in America.

◆◆ If the person has any difficulty in writing. One person may have dyslexia; another, perhaps, a broken arm. If this is the case you will have to look at the writing in a slightly different way. When people have difficulty in reading (as in dyslexia), the rhythm in their writing will be changed and so we do not analyze this movement. When people are ill they may have jerky writing and so it is important that we know this is caused by illness rather than by something else in the personality.

◆◆ If the person is right- or left-handed. Left-handed people sometimes have difficulty slanting their writing in the way they were taught; in that case the altered slant may have a slightly different meaning.

Now you know what is required, but how do you start?

First, decide whether you would like to give people a blank piece of paper so they can write down the answers to these questions or whether you would prefer to design your own special form that they can fill in. One way to do this is shown in the sample on the next page.

Whatever you choose to do, always ask the person to write on unlined paper. If you have designed your own form, make sure there is enough space for the person to write about 10 lines spontaneously (in other words, not copied). Unlined paper is important because studying the baseline (the imaginary line upon which we write) shows how the person was feeling at the time of writing.

Ask the person to write in fountain pen or ballpoint so that you can tell how much energy he or she has from the pressure he or she exerts on the paper. If people write in pencil, felt tip, or a rollerball pen, the true pressure of their writing does not show through the paper.

Ask them to finish by writing his or her normal signature. (The signature is how you see yourself and the writing is how others see you.) If the signature is different from the text, the writer may have difficulty in recognizing him- or herself as he or she really is, so it might be a good idea for a member of his or her family to be there when you give the analysis in case the writer disagrees with what you say.

If he or she cannot think what to write about, suggest that he or she describe his or her hobbies or family, or perhaps you have ideas of your own about what he or she can write. Here's an example of what you can put on your special form:

HANDWRITING SAMPLE FOR ANALYSIS

Please write in your usual writing:

Name:

Age:

Male or female:

Nationality:

Country in which you learned to write:

Are you left- or right-handed?:

Are you dyslexic?:

Please write below on this unlined paper approximately 10 lines on any subject, spontaneously (in other words, not copied) in dark blue fountain pen or black ballpoint. Write your normal signature at the end of this writing sample.

> We drove   up   to
> first   we   went   to
> lunch   and   went   and   put
> field   then   we   had
> quite   early   8:45   and
> breakfast   and   went
> Dartmoor   over   Steam

Here is a movement chart for you to work from. You could either use a highlighter pen or draw a circle around the appropriate movements:

MOVEMENT CHART FOR ANALYSIS

Name of the writer (in case this sheet gets lost, you will know whom it belongs to when you find it again!)

The pen	Thick		Thin	
Width	Wide	Narrow		
Slant	Right	Left	Upright	Mixed
Connected	Connected	Disconnected		
Size	Large		Small	
Zones	Upper	Large	Small	
	Lower	Large	Small	
	Middle	Large	Small	
Baselines	Rising	Falling	Straight	Concave Convex
Spacing	Words	Wide	Narrow	
	Lines	Wide	Narrow	
Regularity	Regular	Irregular (all over the place)		
Rhythm	Flowing	Not flowing		
Pressure	Heavy	Medium	Light	
Style	Simple	Flowery		

You have now completed the first two steps involved in analyzing writing. Here are the following three steps:

●✦ Look up the interpretations for these movements in each chapter. Make a note of what these interpretations are.

●✦ Now turn to the A-Z section at the back of the book and check that there are at least three different movements for each characteristic to make sure you are correct about the writer's personality.

◆▸ Write down all the interpretations that are confirmed by at least three movements.

To see how this analysis is done, look at the example below. First the movement is written, then the interpretation is given. Two more examples of each characteristic, taken from the A-Z section, are given in brackets.

Mixed slant = versatile (disconnected and large size).

Large size = friendly (wide width and large middle zone).

Small upper zone = practical (mixed lower zone and large middle zone). Note: it is unusual for the handwriting to show practicality in all three zones so this is a particularly ingenious writer when it comes to practical problem-solving.

Wide width = open-minded (irregular and large size).

Disconnected = many different ideas (irregular and mixed slant).

Falling baselines. The person was tired at the time of writing so we do not use this movement when we speak to the writer.

Wide word spacing = needs space in which to move about (large size).

Fairly simple style = practical (all individual zones).

Irregular = likes to do things for a short time (wide width).

No rhythm = likes to do things for a short time.

Pressure = lots of energy, likes doing things.

Note: as the pen was neither thick nor thin it is not considered in this analysis and neither is the line spacing because it is a mixture of wide and narrow.

Why Graphology is Fun

Graphology is a hobby that you can study all over the world – wherever you are living or are on holiday, you only need some handwriting, a few tools of the trade, and this book.

Analyzing writing helps you to unlock the mysteries of other people's personalities. You will be amazed at what you can tell by looking at people's writing. Each time you examine someone's writing you will be increasing your analyzing skills.

Why are some people difficult to get on with? Is it just me, or are they impossible for everyone? You can find out by looking at their handwriting.

Anyone who can write can communicate. Think of all the pen pals you might make by writing to people in different countries all over the world. By looking at their writing you can get to know all about their characters while you enjoy what they tell you in their letters.

Your handwriting is a picture of yourself – and you may discover all sorts of good things that you didn't know about yourself by looking at your writing.

Graphology satisfies an inquisitive mind, because the answer to your curiosity about someone is at your fingertips. It helps you to understand your family and friends. Sometimes you want to talk to people but do not know how to do it. By studying their handwriting you can make new friends because you know how to approach them.

Do you really know all the good things about your friends? Look at their writing to discover their hidden qualities.

TOOLS OF THE TRADE FOR THE EAGER BEAVER

Magnifying glass
Fountain pen or ballpoint
Pencil
Eraser
Ruler
Protractor
Paper for making notes
Carbon paper to discover pressure
Scrapbook or file in which to keep everything together

CHAPTER 5

Why Your Writing is the Way it is

Although we learn how to write, we do not copy exactly what we have been taught. Why? The orders that come from the brain send three types of messages: emotional, which is to do with your feelings; intellectual, which affects the way you think; and physical, which describes how you use your energy. We develop our own pattern of writing; even identical twins have different writing!

Look at the two samples of handwriting opposite, written by 12-year-old twins. The letters in the middle zone (such as "n", "a", "e", and "r") look the same because they are similar in size but the shape of the letter "d" is different. Now look at the lower zones (the descenders of letters like "g" and "y") and you will see they are different. Finally, the spaces between the words are completely different.

Although identical twins look the same, they will know that there are differences between them, even if other people cannot see these.

1. do and gets all very clever, he is

2. a while ago she couldn't so determined every day course she won't ever be glebe House now which is a

Q. Why does your writing change?

A. Sometimes we see somebody else write with a movement that we fancy and so we copy that and incorporate it into our own writing. This is called a deliberate change and we hope that it will create a certain effect.

with the kids then I'll go home. and I'll come visit on wednesday

The circular "i" dot in the sample above is a typical deliberate change and shows some creativity.

However, as we grow up other changes also take place in our writing. Although we may be unaware that we are writing differently, we will notice these changes appearing gradually as we create our own unique style of writing.

Q. Are there any other reasons why your writing changes?

A. Yes. Your feelings show up in your writing, so when you are happy you will write more quickly and freely, whereas when you are anxious your writing will become slower because your energy goes inside you to cope with the anxiety.

If you learn about yourself by examining your own writing, you will know that you have studied accurately and can then go on to discover other people's characters correctly.

Knowing yourself will give you self-confidence. How well do you really know yourself? Studying your own writing can help you to discover lots of good points that you may not know you have.

You are very much alive and growing. Only you know whether you are happy with yourself as you are or whether you are ready to change and grow.

Understanding others will help you to make friends and to fit in with groups that you join, such as the Scouts or Guides, the sports team, or the music group.

It is really important to feel good about yourself. When you are having a bad day or feeling blue, it's a great idea to look at all your strengths. Once you have learned about your good points, you can write them down and keep them in a safe place to look at as often as you want. It is also comforting to know that we all have doubts. We all have sad as well as happy days.

While it is important to recognize your good points, it is also wise to know about your weaknesses. You can then decide whether to work on them or to accept them. We all have weaknesses and when we can accept that some people are perhaps better than we are at tennis and maybe others are worse at music, life is easier to understand.

It is infuriating when someone in school is good at everything – but take heart because he or she will have some hidden weakness and by studying his or her writing you may discover new sides to his or her character. You might even find that you are better than he or she is in another area.

The great advantage to studying handwriting is that it can help you to achieve what you really want in life. To be a winner or to reach the goal you have set for yourself involves a lot of hard work, so how can handwriting help?

It can help in many ways. For example, it can show you how to develop determination, willpower, and self-confidence. Would you like to change? If so, are you willing to try a writing exercise for a couple of minutes every morning before breakfast? It will help you to develop your character.

It is important to practice only one exercise at a time because:

◆✦ It does not take much time.

◆✦ You will be more inclined to do it every day.

◆✦ You will achieve each goal more quickly.

Choose ONLY ONE of the following exercises. When you have developed the new character trait, you can stop practicing that particular movement and try another.

In order to keep a record and to show your progress it would be a good idea to work in an exercise book, using one page for each day. Write the date at the end of each exercise. It will be interesting to look back and see how and when your writing and your character changed.

To Improve Your Concentration

To help you to improve your concentration, try drawing the shapes shown in this exercise:

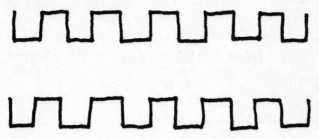

To Relax

Try the following exercise to help you to relax, no matter what is making you feel stressed, overtired, or just in need of a break. Try drawing waves like the ones shown here. Every time your pen makes a downward stroke, make it heavy. Then, when the stroke comes up, make it lighter. If you put your fingers on the other side of the paper, and you are doing the exercise correctly, you will be able to feel the difference between the downstrokes (heavier indentations) and the upstrokes (lighter ones).

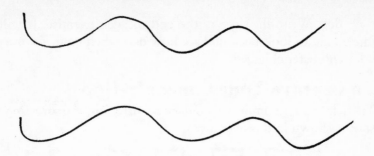

To Feel More Comfortable with People

Are you rather shy? Would you like to feel more at ease with people? If so, try making your writing wider or more broad. Look at the way you write the letter "n" and see if you can give it more space along the baseline (along the bottom of the letter). The first example shows how I used to write and the second one shows how I usually write now. You can see that the writing in the second example is much wider. It will take time, but keep trying and eventually you will feel more comfortable with people.

I enjoy running

I enjoy running

Now you are ready to learn some of the secrets of graphology.

CHAPTER 7

The Pen

Some people are very fussy and will only write with their special pen, whereas others may have a favorite pen but will still be willing to use something else when their own pen is not to hand. Which category do you belong to? We will talk more about this later in the chapter.

Do you prefer to write with a pen that shows plenty of ink on the paper, as in the sample shown below?

> They have hair that shine
> and every one wants to .
> they do. They both have w

Or do you prefer to use a pen that makes a fine stroke on the paper, as in the sample shown below?

> Thomas's uncle Ned was tall b
> His gold watch-chain glittered and I
> He was a little like bold Seacaptain, for
> Since he was a lad. He lived and wo

THICK STROKE

When the fountain pen, felt tip, and various other pens you may like to use show plenty of ink on the paper, we call this a thick stroke. If you like to make a thick stroke, you may enjoy lots of color in your life, perhaps be creative, enjoy mixing with people, and generally be good fun to be around.

List of qualities for thick stroke:

artistic	enjoys travel	outgoing
cheerful	flexible	realistic
creative	friendly	self-assured
easy-going	good mixer	trusting
enjoys being with people	lots of interests	

Hannah loves teddys, Bears, beany babies, 6ft also animal teddy. Her room is allways a tip up by teddys, pencils and

Thick stroke + narrow width + connected = likes to give of his or her best

THIN OR FINE STROKE

If you prefer to see a fine look on the paper (it is called a thin or fine stroke), you will probably like to think deeply about the things that interest you and the people who are important in your life. Sometimes you would like to be more easy-going but find it difficult to relax and enjoy life all the time.

List of qualities for thin stroke:

analytical	industrious	prefers one-to-one contact
hard worker	logical	self-contained
idealistic	observant	thinks deeply

IT is all I can think of doing
but the best way is to
go along in the rehearsal
a term to learn them but
I enjoy it very much

**Thin stroke + connected + large lower zone =
thinks deeply**

Using Any Pen or Ballpoint

Maybe you use any old pen or ballpoint that is near to hand? In this case look at the interpretations for both thick and thin writing. When you see a trait that you think you have, check the A-Z section at the back of the book to see whether you also display the other writing movements for that characteristic, to make sure you are correct in your analysis.

Fascinating Facts

Q. Which pen writes more quickly – the one that makes a broad or thick stroke, or the one that looks fine or thin?

A. Usually the one with a thick stroke, because it flows more easily and often makes less of a mark through the paper. We will talk more about this when we look at how much pressure or energy there is in the writing.

Q. Why can writing with a thick stroke look as though there may be more pressure than writing with a fine stroke?

A. Writing with a thick stroke covers a larger space than writing with a fine stroke. This means that, through a trick of the eye, you can be misled into thinking that the pressure must be heavy as well.

Writing with a thick stroke is called "pasty." This word, which may sound funny to English-speakers, actually comes from the French word *pâteux*. The easiest way for you to understand the meaning is to think of how the toothpaste looks on your brush before you clean your teeth. In this book I shall always call pasty writing thick or thick-stroke because that is easier for you to remember.

Writing with a thin or fine stroke is called sharp, but in this book I have called it fine or thin-stroke to make it easier to remember.

Quiz

Is the writing in the sample shown on the opposite page written with a thick stroke or a fine one?

Puzzle

Look at the sample below again. Is the writer a friendly person?
You can find this out for yourself by checking in the A-Z at the
end of the book to see if his or her writing has some of the other
movements necessary for friendliness.

I hate maths because it
hates it. I can't think of any
elsept for my maths teach
with maths, I hate exept for
Daniel Batter hates maths becau
I mean you arn't exattly gon
and start resiting what you whe
by the way he is sitting next t
the stupidest maths teacher, have

Eager Beaver

Take your magnifying glass and look at the individual strokes
made by your pen in the sample of writing you did before you
started reading this book. Is there:

◆◆ A definite pattern in each stroke?

◆◆ A mixture of patterns in the strokes?

◆◆ A general blob of ink on one of the letters?

◆◆ Anything else?

It is easier to see the pattern of the stroke when the sample has been written in either fountain pen or ballpoint.

Next time you are watching television and see someone using a pen (often famous people are shown signing their name), look to see where he or she holds the pen. People who are more logical tend to hold their pen close to the nib, whereas those who are more artistic in their approach to life tend to hold their pen further up the stem.

Normally people who hold the pen close to the nib exert heavier pressure than those who hold the pen further up the stem. If a writer can make heavy pressure while also holding the pen high up on the stem, that is a very clever person. Which way do you hold your pen?

Width

When we look at the width of the writing, it tells us whether people enjoy adventure and trying out new things. To discover this, we are going to look at the small letter "n." How do you write the letter "n?"

my opinion
st costume.
bright red

Is it wide across the bottom?

name is Hannah. I am
have one brother called
sister called Jennifer. My

Is it narrow across the bottom?

I just want to say
I'm gonna be a
have a pink jeep!

Does the "n" look like a complete square? Drawing a box around the letter can make it easier for you to see the width.

<u>WIDE OR BROAD WRITING</u>

The wider the "n" at the bottom, the more likely it is that the writer will be an enthusiastic person with an open mind and an easy-going manner.

List of qualities for broad width:

easy-going all the time	lively	outgoing
helpful	lots of interests	receptive to new ideas
imaginative	naturally friendly	self-confident
inventive	optimistic	sympathetic

So unique. Their voi
strong and american.
song that they ha
I'll be missing you
Evans. I love Pu

Broad width + disconnected +
large size = imaginative

NORMAL WIDTH

If your "n" fits into a box and looks like a square, we call this normal width. This means that you have the characteristics of both wide and narrow width, so you will have to check all the interpretations to see which ones fit you. It also means that you know when it is all right to be lively and when it is wise to be quiet.

List of qualities for normal width:

easy-going sometimes	good team player	mature
flexible	hard-working	realistic
friendly when appropriate	inclined to compromise	sensible
happy	likes a routine	stable

I really enjoy but I have no
Basketball is the sport I play
time after school at home. I
at home with which I practi.
and ball skills. My dad used to
at school when he was a boy,
has become my coach! He tea
everything I need to know

**Normal width + half-and-half connected +
fairly simplified = enjoys being part of a team**

Narrow Width

If your "n" is narrow at the bottom, you may prefer to concentrate on one thing at a time. Some people like to have one goal in life, so they put all their energy into achieving it. For instance, Pete Sampras would like to become the best tennis player in history and so he devotes all his time to practicing and preparing in order to play as well as he possibly can.

List of qualities for narrow width:

careful	perfectionist	self-disciplined
concentrates well	persistent	single-minded
consistent	scientific	thrifty
controlled	secretive	

When I was very young, something happend

I was riding my tricycle along the path came out of my pocket and rolled on to it I heard a loud hoot. I stoped and ie and bang. When I woke up I had an thing leg. My Mum was standing over

**Narrow width + connected + regular =
likes to work on one task at a time**

Quiz

Look at the sample on the following page. Is the small letter "n" always the same width?

Puzzle
Look again at that sample. Is the writer a shy person?

clock I woke
ent down
Golf Club,
caddying

the member
for started
unfortunate
badly for th

Fascinating Facts

It is very difficult to change the width of your handwriting. You may be able to change the way you write your small letter "n" for a short while, but you will soon find that it reverts to the normal way.

When criminals try to forge other people's writing, one of the ways they are discovered is by examining the width of their writing. The rascal will often write his own "n" when the letter comes near the end of a word. It is difficult for a forger to keep copying something accurately because of the deep concentration needed. All of us have breaks of concentration even though we are trying hard and this is when the forger's own writing takes over from that which he is copying.

Eager Beaver

Which other letter is similar to the "n" and could be used in addition to the "n" to discover the width in someone's writing?

Some people like to pretend that they are open-minded and have no firm views, whereas that isn't really the case. You can discover these types by studying the way they write the letter "n." You will find that nearly all the letters are wide and then suddenly you will spot one or two narrow "n" formations. This will tell you that the writer is putting on an act.

Looking at the sample on the previous page, notice that although the writing is very large, great care has been taken to place the "i" dot precisely over the letter "i." This shows that the writer can have a good eye for detail when he or she is interested in what he or she is doing.

Look carefully to see the way the letter "f" is formed. It has two movements – one straight down-stroke and then the letter "c" is made at the top of the stroke. This highly original formation shows someone who likes to be creative. You might like to see how many different ways people write the letter "f." You could cut out those examples and make a page in your scrapbook or file.

We are all warm and loving. Some of us like everyone to know this (a right slant shows this), while others prefer to keep these feelings to themselves (their writing will normally have a left or upright slant). Which way does your writing normally slant?

This sample shows a right slant.

to play with me on hot Sum
One day my mum told me
ill and had to visit the

This sample shows a left slant.

furnished with blue. It danced on girls, who sat together hemming half finished skirt of the dress

This sample shows an upright slant (as though the upper zone is standing up straight).

team is the team which

getting the ball past the

This sample shows a mixed slant (sometimes to the right, sometimes to the left, and it may even be upright sometimes as well).

are gold and silver but dads house because my that I am not allowe house because they are room for us. So I wi

RIGHT SLANT

If your writing slants to the right, it means that you make friends easily and you are often chatty as well.

List of qualities for right slant:

adventurous	far-sighted	open
courageous	kind	outgoing
energetic	likes to keep options	sociable
enterprising	lively	spontaneous
enthusiastic	loves travel	

Right slant + thick stroke + broad width = enthusiastic

UPRIGHT SLANT

As it is very difficult to write exactly upright (90°) all the time, we will allow the writing to slant to the right or left by a degree or two. If you have an upright slant you may find that you enjoy your independence and that you also have a lot of common sense. You can take responsibility and tend to be practical.

List of qualities for upright slant:

consistent	independent	self-assured
enjoys being part of a team	level-headed	self-controlled
fair	realistic	sensible
inclined to compromise	reliable	stable

David lay quite still in the dar men's low muttering. But this q their voices only as a vague

Upright + thick stroke + large middle zone + narrow
word spacing = enjoys being with people

LEFT SLANT

Writers with a left slant tend to keep their feelings to themselves.
They can be shy and hope that by not expressing their emotions
they will avoid getting hurt too easily. They are also cautious
when making friends, but once they do choose you for a friend
they will be very loyal.

List of qualities for left slant:

cautious	modest	quiet
determined	needs time to be alone	secretive
independent	practical	self-controlled
keeps distance from others	prefers one-to-one contact	

Off-road bikes need thick, knobbly are narrower than on road bikes and of off-road biking. Enduro jagged knob jures good grip on mud and sand. The shock de a thick steel spring. There is oil in the in this oil

Left slant + wide word spacing + small middle zone = prefers
one-to-one contact

MIXED SLANT

When the writing slants first one way and then another, and is generally mixed throughout the sample, it means that these people can turn their hand to many different things. They like lots of variety and prefer to work at tasks that do not take too long to complete.

If you write with a mixed slant you could be very clever, but it may be hard for you to keep going when life becomes too difficult. Try to discuss this with a friend or family member because he or she can help you to recognize some of your many talents and then you may understand how important it is to persist when you really want to succeed.

List of qualities for mixed slant:

adaptable	full of practical ideas	quick-thinking
concentrates in short bursts	likes lots of variety	versatile
flexible	likes to keep options open	lots of interests

Mixed slant + irregular + arrhythmic = individualist

Fascinating Facts

The way that you slant your writing can change quite easily according to how you are feeling and even whom you are writing to. You may write beautifully for your teacher but when dropping a line to a friend your writing may usually be faster and more flowing.

As we can change our slant quite easily, it is important to check that there are at least three other writing movements with the same meaning as the slant before you can be sure the interpretation is correct. Look at the A-Z section at the back of the book for other movements with the same meaning.

Quiz

Is the writing below written with a slant that slopes the same way all the time?

Puzzle

The writer of the sample below has heavy pressure. He or she also has a left slant, so does he or she have a third movement to confirm that he or she is a determined person? Find out by checking in the A-Z section at the back of the book.

Eager Beaver

When you are having difficulty analyzing someone's writing, it is helpful to trace over his or her writing movements to "get under his or her skin." Handwriting comes from the brain, so this method gives you a direct line to the way the writer feels.

Find a ballpoint or pen that has run out of ink (we call this a dead ballpoint or dead pen). Choose three samples of writing – one with a right slant, one with a left slant, and one with a mixed slant. Take the dead ballpoint or pen and, working with one sample of writing at a time, trace over the writing movements for a minute or two. How do your feelings change with each sample? Do you think these emotions reflect those of the writer?

I would like to write
Favourite football club
Supported them since I

Connectedness

Connectedness refers to the number of letters that you join up in each word and tells you about the way you think. It also shows how well you fit in when you are with other people. When writing, how many letters do you join up? Do you:

◆✦ Join up most of your letters?

> *good time. I had my*
> *I had an icecream*

◆✦ Prefer not to join up your letters?

> Said   Sorry   are
> Now   I   like   her
> We   play   together

CONNECTED WRITING

The more writers connects or join up their writing, the more they like to think about and work on one topic at a time. They will often have good concentration but do not like to be disturbed while at work.

List of qualities for connected writing:

cautious	fair	self-disciplined
concentrates well	likes a routine	single-minded
consistent	scientific	steady worker
curious		

and Eric went to a haunted ho
three Darlington Road. They open
there where cobwebs everywhere,
ards made a creaking noise they saw

Connected + regular + heavy pressure = steady worker

DISCONNECTED

This means that most of the letters are not joined up. These writers think in short, sharp bursts and able to hop from one subject to another with ease. They often have an unusual and inventive imagination.

List of qualities for disconnected writing:

artistic	imaginative	mentally agile
creative	likes lots of variety	receptive to new ideas
enterprising	lots of interests	spontaneous
inventive	loves to travel	

America I attend
ipel Christian school
ch, CA I'm visiting
hie. Sophie has

**Disconnected + irregular + some broad width =
variety of interests**

HALF-AND-HALF CONNECTED

This means that you join together some letters in each word. It is
the ideal type of connectedness. It shows that the writer generally has intuitive ideas that are usually followed up in a logical
way. These writers tend to sift through their thoughts with common sense and balance.

List of qualities for half-and-half connected:

balanced approach to people	full of practical ideas	good team
flexible	good all-rounder	player
friendly	good listener	quick-thinking

and tell my tutor
where to contact my
emergencies. At the
in English with Mr
my teacher. She is tal

**Half-and-half connected + fairly broad width +
irregular = practical**

Fascinating Facts

In some types of work people are required to write in a special way. For instance, those who work as draftsmen or printers will probably not join up their writing because when they are at work they have to write the individual letters separately.

Sometimes criminals think it looks more honest if they print instead of joining up their writing!

Quiz

Which is quicker – to write with connected writing or to write each letter separately? Set the timer for one minute and see for yourself. For the first minute write each letter separately. Then set the timer for another minute and this time join up all the letters in each word. Did you write more words during the first or second minute?

Puzzle

Looking at the sample below, does this writer enjoy routine in everyday life?

the Victorian period
toilets in there back

Share your bed with
tell as Itchy bed bug
y make you scbrabch

Eager Beaver

Sometimes letters look as though they have been joined up but in fact they are only touching. The writer has had to lift the pen off the paper and start again in a new position. We call this false connectedness. Look at the sample on page 53 with disconnected + irregular + some broad width = variety of interests. The two "o"s in the word "school" appear to be joined up but, if you look closely, you will see that the pen came off the paper at the top of the first "o" and moved across in the air before being put back on the paper to begin writing the second "o."

See if you can find any more examples where this writer has used false connectedness.

Size

The size of our writing tells us how we feel about ourselves – whether we are bold and like to be noticed or whether we are shy and prefer to stay in the background.

The size of writing is divided into two parts. We have the whole size, which means looking at the tops of the letters "b", "d", "f", "h", "k", "l", and "t", and going to the bottom of such letters as "f", "g", "j", "p", "q", "y", and sometimes "z", depending on how you write that particular letter. To be absolutely precise about knowing which is large, medium and small size, you will need to use a ruler. For large size the writing will be more than 12mm ($^1/_2$in), for medium size it will be 9-12mm ($^3/_8$–$^1/_2$in), and for small size it will be less than 9mm ($^3/_8$in). As people get older their average size of writing tends to become a little smaller. Look at the sample at the top of page 57, which shows you how to measure correctly.

gardening

LARGE SIZE

These people are usually outgoing and very sociable, sometimes oozing confidence in their own abilities, with plenty of imagination and a grand outlook on life. Many actors and actresses have large writing because they enjoy being in the limelight.

List of qualities for large size:

ambitious	excitable	self-confident
bold	flamboyant	sociable
enjoys being with people	imaginative	spontaneous
enterprising	lively	talkative
enthusiastic	optimistic	

been growing up, I've always
I've read her autobiography and
I thought it was really interesting

Large size + rising baselines + heavy pressure
= ambitious

MEDIUM SIZE

These people tend to be realistic, with a good idea of what they are able to undertake and to complete. They are often practical, with a balanced outlook on life. Although they possess some characteristics of writers with both large and small size, they will show these qualities less strongly.

List of qualities for medium size:

compassionate	helpful	practical
conventional	inclined to compromise	prefers action to
dependable	level-headed	reflection
enjoys being part of a team	likes routine	steady worker
happy	likes to conform	trusting

*I am reading a poin
It's about a tennis
and her best maria
killed. After that*

**Medium size + connected + normal word spacing
= enjoys being part of a team**

SMALL SIZE

People who write with small size are modest in nature. They often like to avoid attention by working quietly on their own. They can have a good eye for detail and are precise in whatever they do, thinking things through carefully before acting.

List of qualities for small size:

accurate	controlled	realistic
attends to detail	keeps distance from others	self-sufficient
careful	needs time to be alone	self-contained
cautious	observant	scientific
concentrates well	quiet	

When I was young, something will never forget I punch my when see would boss me attention and one day I ha and tolled me what to do

Small size + connected + wide word spacing = careful

The Zones

Now that we have looked at the whole size, we are going to study the size of the different parts that make up the letters. These are called zones.

If there were such a thing as perfect writing, each zone would be $3\frac{1}{2}$mm ($\frac{1}{8}$in) in size. The difference and variation in the size of each zone is unique to each one of us. The upper zone contains the ascenders or upper stems of the letters "b", "d", "f", "h", "k", "l", and "t". Both upper and lower zone letters have a part that falls into the middle zone. The lower zone contains the descenders or lower stems of the letters "f", "g", "j", "p", "q", "y", and "z" if it has a loop. The remaining letters appear in the middle zone only. They are "a", "c", "e", "i", "m", "n", "o", "r", "s", "u", "v", "w", "x", and "z" if it does not have a loop.

The writing in the sample below shows you a large or tall upper zone, a small middle zone, and a large lower zone.

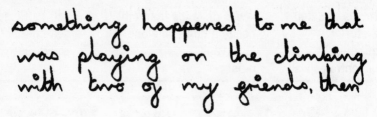

The sample below shows you writing with a large middle zone and a small upper zone.

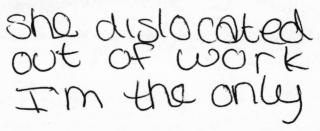

The upper zone represents the writer's aspirations, ideas, and imagination. A person's ideas and imagination can be determined by the size of his or her upper strokes and possibly loops – the larger the upper zone, the more imaginative he or she is likely to be. The middle zone represents a person's practicality and the way he or she can adapt to everyday life. It is also ego-related and shows how people react socially – the larger the middle zone, the chattier they are likely to be. The lower zone represents the writer's material approach to life, his or her degree of physical energy and his or her attitude towards the basic needs of life. The longer the lower zone, the more time the writers will spend searching for a place to call home where they can put down roots. Safety and a sense of security will often be important to him or her in all aspects of life.

LARGE UPPER ZONE

The larger the upper zone, the more ideas the writer will have. Some of these will be good (with normal loops) while others will be more dreamlike with huge hoops. He or she may also be ambitious and know what he or she wants to do in the future.

List of qualities for large upper zone:

ambitious	far-sighted	idealistic	intellectual

The dinosaurs lived on
age. Even the best scien
made the dinosaurs die

**Large upper zone + wide line spacing + right slant
= far-sighted**

SMALL UPPER ZONE

The smaller the upper zone, the more practical the writer is. He or she will not worry about what he or she will be doing in a few years' time – he or she places more importance on living in the here and now.

List of qualities for small upper zone:

realistic	self-reliant	sociable

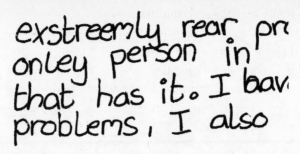

exstreemly rear pr
onley person in pr
that has it. I bav
problems, I also

Small upper zone + disconnected + thick stroke
= practical

LARGE MIDDLE ZONE

A large middle zone usually means that the writers love being
with people. They may enjoy talking for rather too long on the
telephone! Their social life is important and they would never
choose to live on a desert island!

List of qualities for large middle zone:

enjoys being with people	friendly	practical	realistic

Usually, if a writer has a small upper zone he or she also has a
large middle zone. This is why the interpretations for both the
small upper zone and the large middle zone are so similar. If you
look at the sample for the small upper zone you will see that it
could also be used to illustrate the large middle zone.

SMALL MIDDLE ZONE

A small middle zone usually means that these writers feel rather
shy when they are with people. If he or she has large upper and
lower zones as well, he or she hides his or her shyness and others
often cannot tell how this person feels inside.

List of qualities for small middle zone:

concentrates well	intellectual	shy
hard worker	quiet	

I found a really great room
I had big windows
the back garden. Sunlight

Small middle zone + connected + narrow width
= concentrates well

LARGE LOWER ZONE

The larger the lower zone, the more the writers enjoy deep conversations on the meaning of life. They may also be very concerned about putting down roots and finding a place where they feel safe. When dealing with problems they may like to dig deep to discover the cause rather than simply finding a quick-fix solution.

List of qualities for large lower zone:

energetic	organizing ability	thinks deeply

them down. I like reeding but
spell very well. It anoying.
to write good peeces of wor
get a very low pesin tashun
Its anoying I wish I was

Large lower zone + fine stroke + connected = thinks deeply

SMALL LOWER ZONE

Often if there is a small lower zone the writer has a large middle
zone, so many of the interpretations for a large middle zone
apply. The writer enjoys being with people and chatting to them.
He or she may also be practical and like finding quick-fix solu-
tions to problems.

List of qualities for small lower zone:

| independent | practical | sociable |

---

another game. This game is
World. In this game you have got
and his friends and defeat Bow
You start at yoshi's house. There

**Small lower zone + close word spacing + thick stroke
= friendly**

Fascinating Facts

The size of the whole writing is one of the easiest movements to
change. For instance, if you have large writing you will automat-
ically make it smaller to fit the space available when you are
writing a postcard.

No one can naturally and spontaneously produce zones that
are balanced in all three areas. There is always at least one dominant zone.

If you look at your own writing you will also notice that,
although the size may appear to be the same in one zone, there
will be slight differences. Unlike the computer, we cannot condi-
tion ourselves to produce exactly the same movement all the time.

Quiz

There is one letter in the English alphabet that can go into all three zones. Which one is it?

Puzzle

Looking at the sample below, can the writer concentrate well? This writer has heavy pressure.

When I was very young, something happened to me which
I was playing cricket with my brother, we had got one
cricket sets the stumps were very sharpe so that they
with ease, anyway we started playing with the low
which was dyed red to get that cricket ball look.
We got into an argument like brothends, and my brother

Eager Beaver

Some people write with extremes of size. The largest writing I have found is about 50mm (2in). I wonder if you can find anyone who writes any larger than that?

At the other end of the scale, some people have tiny writing. See what is the smallest whole size in writing that you can find. I once found someone whose size was under 2mm ($\frac{1}{16}$in) – I had to get out my magnifying glass to read the writing!

CHAPTER 12

Baselines

Do you remember that the sample for an analysis has to be written on unlined paper? In this chapter, you are going to learn the reason for this.

Baselines are the imaginary horizontal lines that run across the page. Each time you write a line on plain paper you create your own individual baseline. There are many different types of baseline because this important movement shows what mood we are in when we are writing and also how that affects our behavior.

Sometimes it can be difficult to see exactly what sort of baseline has been made. Here are some suggestions on how to examine the baseline:

◆✦ Turn the writing upside down.

◆✦ Turn over the paper and look at the writing from the reverse side.

◆✦ Turn the writing sideways and look down the baseline from left to right.

◆✦ Hold a plastic ruler against the baseline.

Sometimes your baseline will change as you write. For example, if you are writing a letter to a friend and telling him or her some good news, you may become happier as you write. Your baseline may start to rise and you may not notice this until you have finished the letter.

Let's now look at some of the different baselines we make when we write on unlined paper with no criblines. The black lines will show you the different baselines in the sample below.

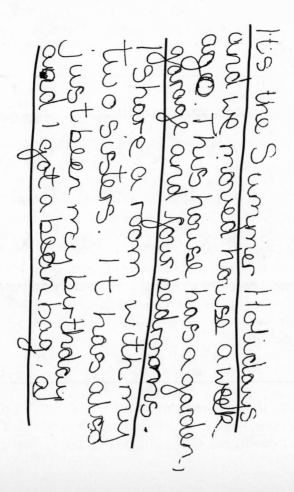

STRAIGHT BASELINES

These people are usually straightforward, reliable, and determined. They have clear aims and know they will achieve what
they set out to do. They are keen to see justice done and people
treated fairly.

List of qualities for straight baselines:

calm	hard-working	self-controlled
concentrates well	independent	straightforward
determined	reliable	trustworthy
fair		

*Socks come in all shapes and
being multi - coloured and some
to make them more attractive
buy them. Most socks have*

Straight baselines + regular + connected = dependable

WAVY BASELINES

A wavy baseline wanders all over the place and each writer may
have several types of wavy baseline in the same sample. Sometimes when people are not feeling well they write with a wavy
baseline, so it is important to collect several samples of writing
from the same person before deciding definitely that they do
have wavy baselines.

These people tend to make decisions according to how they are feeling at the time, so they can sometimes change their mind from one day to the next! They enjoy doing many different things.

List of qualities for wavy baselines:

active mind	likes to keep options open	versatile
likes change		

different types of hobbies, sports. I enjoy softball, ba... tics, and American footba... ...ding fantasy and novel e...

**Wavy baselines + right slant + flowery writing
= likes to keep options open**

RISING BASELINES

These writers are usually optimistic, enthusiastic, and ambitious. Sometimes they can get carried away by their excitement and become impatient. They like to achieve goals quickly so that they can move on to the next target.

List of qualities for rising baselines:

ambitious	energetic	good-humored
bold	enterprising	persevering
cheerful	enthusiastic	prefers action to reflection

and Dad both like

of this I have grown

Rising baselines + large size + heavy pressure = ambitious

FALLING BASELINES

Often young people have falling baselines because it is hard work growing up and so you use up all your energy without realizing it. This means that sometimes you do not realize how tired you are, so if you find yourself with falling baselines perhaps a little more sleep will help you to have more energy.

CONCAVE BASELINES (CURVED BASELINES)

A concave baseline falls at the beginning of the line and then rises again at the end of the line. This type of baseline can be difficult to see. Perhaps if you imagine a cave falling in that will help you to remember what a concave baseline looks like. To help you to see a concave baseline, you may find it is easiest to turn the paper over and upside down. This will help your eye to focus on the baseline because you won't be distracted by the words.

These people tend to be slow starters. They seem to think that they do not want to perform a task, but when they start work they realize it is fun, then they feel good as their confidence grows and so they enjoy finishing the activity.

I have just rang but you we
I have some excecallent news
m the gold meadel for com
race, last night in the C
and at the Olimpus
when I came first. I'm
· you the medal
on to show the any and I
y How are you doing? I
wanted to tell you that
I mostly spend my time
crlcing out. Love you.

Concave baselines + left slant + a mix of narrow and
broad widths = will gain enthusiasm once he or she
gets going on the task

CONVEX BASELINES (ARCHED BASELINES)

The writing goes up at the beginning of the line and then comes
down at the end of the line. Think of an archway, which may
help you to remember what a convex baseline looks like. It is the
opposite of a concave baseline.

These people tend to be full of enthusiasm at first. However, once
they start work they soon realize that they have taken on too much
and become too tired to finish the task they have started. These individuals will find it helpful to think carefully and to take on activities
that only last for a short time. This will allow them to finish what
they start and also to rest before going on to something new.

I remember when I first came to Bohunt. I was scared that people might make fun of me because I'm so short for my age. I used to spend time with Em, my ex-best friend, I thought she'd look after me, but she found someone else, and I had no one. It's all right now, though, I have lots of friends, actually I get on with most of the tutor group.

Convex baselines + thick stroke + half-and-half connected = likes lots of short activities

Fascinating Facts

Some people prefer to use lined paper or to put a cribline under the plain paper on which they are writing to help them to make a straight baseline. Even though they do this, they cannot always follow the lines!

Do you ever say or do something and then later on wonder why on earth you behaved so badly? This is when our feelings become so strong that they control our behavior for a short time. That is why we also sometimes have difficulty in writing a straight baseline on unlined paper – our emotions are controlling us.

Quiz

Why is it important to see several samples of someone's handwriting before deciding which is the writer's true baseline?

Eager Beaver

Since the baseline has so much to do with our feelings, it is wise to collect several samples of handwriting from each person over a period of time. This will give you a true picture of the moods and behavior patterns of each individual. Keep a file of handwriting samples that you wish to analyze, then add more samples from the same person as and when you can.

If the baseline is usually the same, the writer's feelings always produce the same sort of behavior. However, if there are lots of different types of baseline, the writer will behave differently according to the mood of the moment.

Some people, even when using lined paper, cannot follow the lines! Try writing on lined paper yourself. Set the timer for two minutes or write on a large sheet of lined paper. When you have finished, look carefully to see if you have used the lines correctly all the time. Try this out on your friends, but do not tell them why you want them to write a whole page using lined paper.

Geri is a leo, and she wants.

lots of people to enjoy the bands

adventure, and even take some encourag-

ment that females really, really

can do it for them selves.

Geri was born in Watford on the

6th August 1972, with a Swedish dad

and a Spanish mum.

Geri is an aerobics instructor,

a dancer and a T.V. presenter in

Turkey.

Puzzle

Is the above writer a hard worker? He or she has heavy pressure.

CHAPTER 13

Spacing between Words and lines

The spacing between the words shows how we communicate best with other people. Some of us like to be surrounded by friends all day, while others need time to be alone and prefer one-to-one contact whenever they feel like being sociable.

To find out what sort of word spacing the writer has chosen, look at the size of the letter "n." When the word spacing is normal, one letter "n" will fit between each word. Look at the sample below.

ement that females
can do it for the
Geri was born
6th August 1972, with
and a Spanish mum
Geri is an a

Wide or large word spacing means that the writer's letter "n" will fit into the spaces several times, as you can see from the sample below.

My hobby is going
Because I like helping
in need of help. Going

Close or narrow word spacing means that there is no room for the writer's letter "n" to fit between each word. Look at the sample below.

I like sewing, but I often don'
time to finish off big sewing
About twice a year, usually
and Summer Holidays, I clear
box and finish off any projects.

WIDE SPACING BETWEEN WORDS

The wider the spaces between the words, the more these writers enjoy being on their own, thinking things over carefully before making decisions.

List of qualities for wide word spacing:

cautious	needs time to be alone	prefers one-to-
keeps distance from others	orderly	one contact
musical	organizing ability	secretive

Wide word spacing + left slant + small size = cautious

NORMAL SPACING BETWEEN WORDS

These writers usually fit in easily with all types of people because they enjoy communicating with others. They know when to talk and when to listen. Generally, they are friendly and reliable individuals. Often they also have plenty of self-confidence.

List of qualities for normal word spacing:

balanced approach to people	helpful	mature
flexible	intelligent	realistic
graceful	loving	stable emotionally

The Beech is fou
throughout the British I:
less common in the Nortl
is often planted in the :

Normal word spacing + thick stroke + large middle zone =
friendly

NARROW SPACING BETWEEN WORDS

These writers are usually well-meaning, with a kind and spontaneous nature. They can also be rather chatty because they love
being with other people.

List of qualities for narrow word spacing:

active	kind	trusting
enjoys being with people	outgoing	well-meaning
impulsive	talkative	

My cat is called muffin. He's a bit of a funny cat k
almost anything except catfood, but he's very frien
very goodmannered rabbit called Gorgie. My favr
is looking after horses and riding them — when I tell
favriot bnimal but I end up telling them all the an
I like them all.

Narrow word spacing + thick stroke + connected
= talkative

SPACING BETWEEN THE LINES

The spacing between the lines tells us how a person's mind works. Normal line spacing means that the writer's ideas are realistic, concrete, and well-defined. Generally speaking, the wider the line spacing the more idealistic the person; the closer the line spacing the more impulsive the writer is likely to be, wanting to act upon ideas immediately.

How do you tell if the line spacing is wide or narrow? For wide line spacing, there will be a clear space between each line. Look at the sample below.

> Saul was still carrying out this
>
> of Jesus, he was on his way to I
>
> shone on him, he heard a vocie

When the line spacing is close, there will be a small space between each line.

> in five days with our remaining men but it is
> We lost many to win this country. It was qui
> was somewhere else and came to us exhaus
> them anyway. They had very few men and
> Are Our archers were stronger and more accu

Sometimes the tails of the "f", "g", "j", "p", "q", "y", and perhaps "z" in one line will touch the tops of the "b", "d", "f", "h", "k", "l", and "t" in the line below. We call this mingling lines and it usually means that the writer has so many ideas it is difficult choosing which one to work on first. The sample below shows mingling lines.

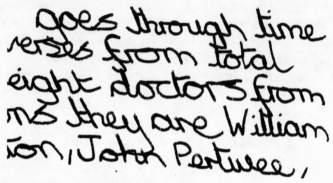

WIDE SPACING BETWEEN THE LINES

These writers are often cautious. They like to find out the facts before they make a decision. They are able to picture the way their plans and ideas will look when completed.

List of qualities for wide line spacing:

cautious	good planner	self-assured
clear thinking	intellectual	thorough
far-sighted	orderly	

Sarah walked slowly through

colossal horse. She halted him

him into the stable and unt

Wide line spacing + upright slant + connected
= clear thinking

NARROW SPACING BETWEEN THE LINES

These writers may be impulsive and lively. There is often a desire to try out any new idea that comes to mind immediately!

List of qualities for narrow line spacing:

concentrates in short bursts	spontaneous
creative	well-meaning

Narrow line spacing + large middle zone + arrhythm
= spontaneous

NORMAL SPACING BETWEEN THE LINES

This is the ideal. These writers have the ability to organize their daily routine and normally have a consistent approach to life. They are an asset in the work environment because their qualities include integrity, common sense, practicality, and level-headedness.

List of qualities of normal line spacing:

clear thinking	open-minded	practical
good leader	organizing ability	realistic
good planner	possesses integrity	self-confident
level-headed	intelligent	tolerant

I am playing the pa
dormouse in the Mad H
It is great fun playing thi
thrilled I have been picked
working with my friends.
new teacher. She is ful

Normal line spacing + regular + wide word spacing
= good planner

Eager Beaver

Sometimes when you look at the spacing between the lines they will appear to mingle. Actually, the tops of the letters from one line and the tails from the other line are very cleverly not touching at all. We call this dovetailing.

You will see some examples of this on the next page (the same one that we are using for the quiz), where the "y" in the word "play" on the fourth line actually sits next door to the "t" in the word "Manchester" on the fifth line. This shows someone who is clever. Another example can be seen in line two, where the "f" of "football" does not touch the "y" of "hobby" in line one. A third example is in line three, where the same "f," but this time its lower zone, misses the "k" in the word "think." Can you spot anywhere else in the sample where this happens?

Quiz
Looking at the sample below, how would you describe the word spacing?

Puzzle
In the sample below, does the writer express himself clearly?

hobby is ...
is football because
think the best footballer
David Cave. I play fool
I support Manchester
team is the best.
for Manchester United
in midfield.
Manchester United
David Beckham
ted.

Fascinating Facts

Every time you write on a piece of paper you choose how to use the space (although you will not be aware of this). It doesn't matter whether you are writing in English, Russian, or Japanese, you will still use the space in a particular way.

Think of the piece of paper as the world and your writing as how you see yourself in the world. The more empty space there is around your writing (between the words and lines, and also the margins), the more you enjoy observing people; and the more writing there is on the paper (perhaps with no margins at all), the more you enjoy being in the middle of the world and having your say.

When we write we are not aware what sort of space we are making on the paper, so it is very difficult to alter the way we arrange our words and lines.

This means that the spacing we make on the paper is an important factor in helping to identify a forger. That's because although a good forger may perfect the loops and flourishes of someone else's writing, he will unconsciously apply his own style of word spacing and eventually, when a reasonable length of text is involved, this will catch him out.

The same principle can apply in the case of identifying the writer of anonymous letters. However carefully the writing may be disguised or altered, the word spacing can be an incriminating factor.

As you need to see the space between each line, it is important to have enough lines to study. This is why it is best to ask for a full page of writing when you are going to do an analysis.

Regularity

The regularity of our writing tells us about the amount of self-discipline we have – or perhaps do not have! It also shows how practical and persevering we can be.

What we are looking for in regular writing is an overall picture that shows uniformity. It may help you to think of soldiers marching or perhaps a flowerbed where all the flowers have been planted very carefully in lines, with exact spaces between each plant. To understand what I mean, look at the sample below which shows regular handwriting.

Dinosaurs lived on
million years. They
Era which was

Now look at this sample of irregular handwriting.

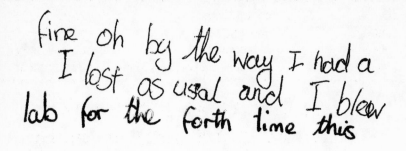

Now that you have seen a sample of both regular and irregular writing, what sort of writing do you have? If you have difficulty deciding because your writing is nearly regular but is also slightly irregular, then look at the following factors:

●✦ The size of the letters – especially those that use the middle zone ("a", "c", "e", "i", "m", "n", "o", "r", "s", "u", "v", "w", "x", and sometimes "z"). In regular writing, these will be the same size. In irregular writing, the letters will vary in size.

●✦ The spaces between the words. In regular writing, there will be the same sized space between the words. In irregular writing, the size of the spaces between the words will vary.

●✦ The slant of the writing. In regular writing, all the letters will have the same slant. In irregular writing, the letters will slant in different directions.

REGULAR WRITING

The more regular your writing, the more self-control you have and use. You will enjoy working to a routine and like to know what you have to do. You are usually a steady worker and a reliable member of a team.

List of qualities for regular writing:

calm	conventional	orderly
cautious	dependable	reliable
concentrates well	determined	self-disciplined
consistent	enjoys being part of a team	single-minded

I have been reading a book called of Thomas Covenent) It was written by called Thomas covenant who is on a friendly giants and some loyal friends the one tree. He then sets sail again against the sunbane who send

Regular + connected + narrow width = consistent

IRREGULAR WRITING

The more irregular your writing, the more flexible and creative you are in your approach to life. You often have quite strong feelings that you like to share with others.

List of qualities for irregular writing:

active mind	spontaneous excitable	inventive
adventurous	flexible	likes to keep options open
artistic	idealistic	lots of interests
enjoys travel	imaginative	optimistic
enterprising	individualist	practical
enthusiastic	informal	spontaneous

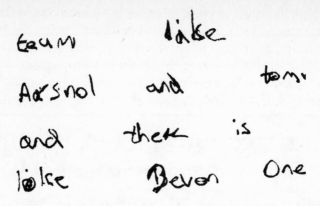

Irregular + disconnected + arrhythmic = individualist

Fascinating Facts

People don't write absolutely regularly, because if they did they'd be robots! We are all unique and so there will be some movements that we do in our own individual way. Therefore, no matter how regular the writing looks, there will still be small irregularities in some of the movements.

Quiz

Which is quicker – to write with regular writing or to write with irregular writing?

Which person would be more flexible and willing to change his or her plans – a person with regular writing or someone with irregular writing?

Puzzle

Does the writer in the following sample prefer to work to a routine or does he or she prefer short bursts of different activities?

Eager Beaver

Although we are taught how to write our letters, not one of us is

able to create an exact copy of what we have been taught. In the
olden days when only the monks were taught to write, they used
the italic script. Even so, each monk had his own unique way of
writing. Next time you look at the writing of people from earlier
times – perhaps in a history book, an old book in a museum, or
a Bible in a church – look to see how the handwriting differs
from person to person.

Write to someone you admire telling him or her why you like
him or her. When he or she replies, take a dead pen (one in
which the ink has run out) and trace his or her writing. This will
give you a sense of his or her personality.

I Like all types of mu
band is Status Quo
realy get you moveing.
what ever you want. I
songs on my core
some songs to my dad
like them exopt in
know what songs sl
2 to 3 tapes of these

CHAPTER

15

Rhythm

Rhythm is about the flow of life. We all have our ups and downs, our happy and sad times. The rhythm of our writing shows how we cope with our thoughts and feelings.

To help you to recognize rhythm in handwriting, think of a row of ballet dancers. They are all performing the same movements and yet the way in which each dancer makes those movements is slightly different. Perhaps one girl lifts her toes slightly higher than her neighbor. Maybe someone else points her fingers more than the others. Overall, you do not notice these little differences because you see a peaceful, flowing scene. Here is a sample of fairly rhythmic writing.

I like reading because
relaxing to do.
authers are oick

When there is little or no rhythm in the writing we call it arrhythmic. The movements tend to be jerky or awkward, without any flow. This sample shows arrhythm.

Likes hunting and
Upset and Waves

Now look at your own writing. It may help to hold it at arm's length, so you can see the shape of the words without being distracted by the words themselves. Rhythmic writing will be generally pleasing to the eye and will flow along the page.

RHYTHM
The more rhythm that people have in their writing, the happier they are in themselves. They enjoy life to the full, balancing work and pleasure, self-control with spontaneity, and they have an easy-going attitude towards others.

List of qualities for rhythmic writing:

calm	musical	sensible
consistent	patient	tolerant
happy	self-assured	well-meaning
mature	self-contained	

and also lots of
for shading us from
also good water bar
a lot of water
when it is raining.

Rhythm + right slant + thick stroke = easy-going

Arrhythm

Arrhythmic writing may belong to those who are feeling stressed or who are trying too hard. If this describes you, you may find that it helps to plan your life so that you can balance your work and spare-time activities. Otherwise, there may be times when you work too hard and others when you play too much.

List of qualities for arrhythmic writing:

creative	likes lots of variety	lots of interests
excitable	likes to keep options open	sensitive
individualist		

that is really annoyingbecau
one. The medicine I had t
the sun or heat for to long

Arrhythm + disconnected + thick stroke = creative

Quiz

Rhythm is one of the movements that you make whatever language or script you write in. What other movement can also be used for analyzing writing, no matter whether it is Chinese, Arabic, Hebrew or German.

Puzzle

Is the writer in the sample below self-disciplined?

At the weekend I go runni
We run down the river
We go shopping at tesco
us an hour and a half.
1.00 and I help put away
Sit down for 20 minutes
Then I have lunch, then I
my friends until 6.30.
dinner and get changed

Puzzle

Is the writer in the sample below self-disciplined?

Fascinating Facts

You cannot sign your signature in exactly the same way every time, because the rhythm pattern you make is so unique that there are minute changes each time you put pen to paper.

Rhythm is difficult to produce while you are growing up. It has been very difficult to finding handwriting samples with rhythm for this book, because all the samples belong to children and adolescents.

Eager Beaver

Each person produces his or her own writing pattern. Rhythm is created when this pattern is repeated naturally and spontaneously at intervals and the overall design is balanced and harmonious.

Listen to two people playing the same piece of music. You will hear the same tune but the rhythm will be slightly different in each case. That is because each of us interprets rhythm in a unique way.

Try writing your signature six times in a row and see how many small changes you notice.

CHAPTER
16

Pressure

The pressure of our writing on the page tells us about the energy that we have and how we use it. It is a vital part of handwriting analysis, but you can assess it only when working with original writing. In other words, photocopies, photographs, or reproductions of someone's writing are no good because you cannot feel the indentations that his or her pen makes on the page.

Each time your pen touches the paper, the ink leaves a mark on one side of the paper. If you turn over the paper you will find an indentation that shows the amount of pressure you have used to write. Your hand may move over the paper with a light, delicate touch, or perhaps you put all your weight down on it heavily. This is how you learn to recognize pressure:

◆◆ Take three sheets of white plain paper and two sheets of carbon paper. It may be easier if the plain paper and the carbon paper are the same size.

◆✦ Slip a sheet of carbon paper between each two sheets of plain paper, to make a top copy plus two copies. The order of the papers will be plain paper, carbon paper, plain paper, carbon paper, plain paper. Make sure that the shiny side of the carbon paper is face downwards.

◆✦ Take two paperclips and place one on each side at the top of the papers so that the five layers are held together neatly.

◆✦ Write a sentence in ballpoint on the top copy.

◆✦ Check to see whether one or both of the plain sheets of paper shows your writing.

◆✦ Ask your friends, family, and neighbors to write the same sentence below yours. When the page is full, take each sentence in turn and note on how many of the pages the writing has come through.

If the writing only shows on the top copy, the writer has light pressure. If the writing also shows on the second piece of white paper, the writer has medium pressure. If the writing shows through the two pieces of carbon on to the third sheet of white paper, the writer has heavy pressure.

LIGHT PRESSURE

People with light pressure often prefer to fit in with others because they have no desire to cause trouble. They become tired more easily than those with heavy pressure, but they also tend to be much more delicate and considerate in their approach to life.

List of qualities for light pressure:

adaptable	concentrates in short bursts	intuitive
alert	friendly	mentally agile

MEDIUM PRESSURE

This shows an average amount of energy. Anyone with this pressure will probably have a balanced outlook that enables them to cope happily with the people and situations they meet in everyday life.

If the pressure is medium-light, look at the interpretations for light pressure and adjust them according to the other movements in the writing. If the pressure is medium-heavy, apply the interpretations for heavy pressure if there are sufficient supporting movements.

List of qualities for medium pressure:

balanced approach to people	easy-going	stable
calm	dependable	steady worker
consistent		

HEAVY PRESSURE

This shows that there is a healthy degree of energy. These writers are often emotional, impulsive, and more interested in actions than thoughts. They are doers who may also enjoy working with their hands, and are often pioneers. However, check that the pressure is not too heavy, because in this case the writer will be suffering from too much stress and using up nervous energy.

List of qualities for heavy pressure:

---

ambitious	enterprising	prefers action to reflection
bold	enthusiastic	reliable
concentrates well	flamboyant	self-disciplined
determined	hard worker	thinks deeply
energetic		

Fascinating Facts

When you become angry, you will find that you write with heavier pressure. When you feel happy, very often your pressure will become lighter because you use less energy when you are having fun.

Quiz

Why is there no sample of pressure in this book?

Puzzle

Which person would become tired more easily – someone with light pressure or someone with heavy pressure?

Almost all the writing samples used in this book have been written by different people. However, one person's writing has been used in two different places. Can you find these two samples?

Eager Beaver

Take a piece of paper with writing on one side only. Hold it in your hand, then close your eyes and feel the side of paper on which there is no writing. The more pressure you can feel through the paper, the heavier the writer's pressure.

The style of our writing tells us about the different ways we can be creative. Some of us are practical, whereas other people prefer to have large and colorful ideas that may take time to put into action. As we have discovered, although we are taught to write in a certain way, none of us follows exactly the copybook that we were taught. Some of us add loops and even curls to our writing, while others simplify the letters as much as possible. The way in which we alter the copybook that we were taught is called style.

Simplified writing means that you form only the essential parts to the letters. Look at this sample:

Amy is my pet dog
old. She is a crossbreed
cross red setter and she

Flowery writing means that you add some loops or extra parts to the letters. Look at this sample:

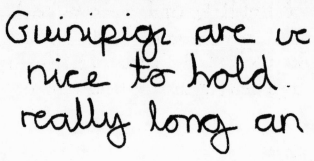

Guinipigz are ve
nice to hold.
really long an

I wonder which sort of style you have? Does your writing look similar to the copybook you were taught? As your character changes, so will your writing style. You may not notice the differences at first, but when going through your scrapbook in years to come you will see the changes and how your personality has altered at certain times in your life.

COPYBOOK

If your writing does look quite similar to the way you were taught, it means that you feel most happy when you know what plan you are following. You love to follow the school timetable and when you are at home you like to know the arrangements for the weekend in advance.

List of qualities for copybook style:

calm	conventional	needs a routine
consistent	enjoys being part of a team	stable

Africa is a big continent of wildlife and various parks and protection. People go there to look at the animals. They h problems because animals are

Copybook + narrow width + regular = needs a routine

SIMPLIFIED

These people are likely to be independent spirits, objective, and intelligent thinkers with the ability to see the essentials of any situation. They enjoy solving practical problems.

List of qualities for simplified style:

active mind	fair	quick-thinking
clear thinking	full of practical ideas	realistic
concentrates well	good organizer	self-sufficient
decisive	mature	scientific
enterprising	mentally agile	straightforward

If I could fly I would Island in the world,) and I view and see just how My best friend was Ali

Simplified + half-and-half connected +
normal line spacing = practical

FLOWERY

These people like bright colors, perhaps visiting famous houses which contain many beautiful things to look at and admire. They often have a lively imagination and lots of original ideas. They are sociable and easy-going, getting on well with others. If the writing is too flowery their ideas may be rather over the top!

List of qualities for flowery style:

artistic	flamboyant	kind
cheerful	friendly	sentimental
easy-going	imaginative	varied interests
enthusiastic		

English is very interes- tied when I get to the of stairs. Maths is okay, but another 4 flights of

Flowery + thick stroke + large middle zone = imaginative

Fascinating Facts

Style of writing is rather like fashion in clothes and furniture. It comes and goes, changing with the times. In England the copybook style was altered in the 1950s from having curves and loops to a more simplified writing with straight up and down strokes.

Although people sometimes imagine that graphology looks at the beauty and legibility of handwriting, you may now realize that there are many other aspects to consider and it could be easy to make a mistake by looking only at the style.

Opinions on style vary. If you have simplified writing, you may not like the look of someone's flowery writing. The person with flowery writing may think that the simplified writing is too bare and that something is missing from it. Deciding on writing style can cause arguments, so it is wiser to agree to disagree sometimes!

Eager Beaver

Think of someone you know who likes wearing clothes that are way out and full of bright and varied colors. Ask him or her to write something for you – you may discover that he or she has extra loops or curls in his or her writing. He or she probably also likes to write with a thick stroke.

If you disagree with someone as to whether his or her writing is simplified or flowery, ask him or her to write his or her letters in the way that he or she was taught at school. Then take another look at the writing under debate to see whether there are extra flowery bits or not.

Next time you are in a library or a bookshop, go to the section on handwriting and see if there are books on the different ways that children are taught to write in various countries all over the world. You will be amazed to see so many different copybook styles.

Quiz

Can anyone write in exactly the same way that he or she was taught to write?

Puzzle

Look at the writing in the sample below. Is the writer consistent?

I am not very lucky
Self or burn My self bu
Understands and I also
I hope to face that as
Deane chivertor hope to
ream and I will be
number will be 13 unluc
for Me !!! We will
and have Madal con
ears and then fix
We all like More
We all want ro

Different Ways in Which Graphology is Used

Graphology can help you to choose a career when you are leaving school, university, or even seeking a new profession later on in life. Graphology is used to help people in all the examples below:

◆✦ **Recruitment** Helping to put individuals into the right jobs where they will enjoy their work and also get on with their team-mates.

◆✦ **Career guidance** Looking at different types of work that could be suitable but which you may not have thought about.

◆✦ **Compatibility between people** Looking at a person's strengths and areas of possible conflict so that these can be discussed and sorted out before, rather than after, problems arise.

◆✦ **Police** Determining whether anonymous letters or forgeries have been written by one or more suspects.

◆◆ **Health**   When you are ill it is always important to go to the doctor. However, handwriting can also reveal signs of ill health.

Practical and Positive Applications

Sometimes we find it difficult to get on with people – they appear uncommunicative, stubborn, or plain hard work! After analyzing our writing we can gain an idea of how to change ourselves so that we can operate on the same wavelength as others. Some of us are highly logical and need to have an explanation for everything, whereas others simply rely on hunches. Some of us like to plan well ahead, while others prefer to do things on the spur of the moment. When we understand how those around us operate we can see how to get on better with them.

Looking at the interpretations for our own handwriting we can decide whether we are happy with the characteristics that we see or whether we would like to change or develop particular personality traits. It can be difficult to believe that we act in certain ways. Sometimes we need our friends to convince us that the meaning of our handwriting is correct! We can also work on improving ourselves; for instance, feeling better about ourselves, working on our self-confidence. As we grow and change, so our writing will develop into our own individual style.

We may know our weaknesses but need help to work through them. Someone older, whom we can really trust, can help us in doing this. Look at the sample of writing opposite. This belongs to a female counsellor who enjoys and is good at helping people. Some of her movements include a right slant, rhythm, and half-and-half connected. These signs show that she is a good listener with an understanding of other people, and also that she has a lot of patience.

Then we bought my present-
with a large sitting room with
oak sill running round
we added two rooms to
[...] being there. It faces
with an acre of largely
a stream running through
a friendly house, and, like
[...] holds a whole range
a place where I feel

CHAPTER 19

Careers

People who do the same work often appear to write in the same way, even though they may be totally different in character. However, the graphologist Robert Saudek (whom we talked about in chapter 2) says that only non-graphologists think that the handwriting of people in the same profession looks very similar.

Just because this chapter shows you the writing of people who are good at their work, it does not mean that these are the only types of writing found in people who are good at their jobs. They are simply examples. In fact, if you look at the next two samples, both these people are good at their jobs and yet their writing is totally different. This shows that there is no perfect writing for a particular job. What is important is that each person has the right characteristics to make him or her good at his or her work. Each of them has put these movements together to form his or her own unique writing pattern.

Saudek says that in the whole human race there are not two individuals who have the same writing, just as there are not two identical oak leaves in existence.

Since this is a book about handwriting analysis, I thought you might like to see a couple of examples of graphologists' writing.

The sample below has a right slant, rhythm, mainly connected writing, normal line spacing, and mainly normal word spacing which is a little wide from time to time. This lady has a balanced approach to life which means that she can plan and organize, use her common sense and also become an eager beaver when she has to spend more time investigating the depths of someone's personality.

> *Having her here has at pleasure: we have a happy, stimulating week. There is never*

The next sample shows another graphologist's writing. At first glance the two writings may look quite alike because they both have a right slant, mainly connected writing, and normal line spacing. However, in this second sample, the word spacing is slightly wider and there is less rhythm. There is a lot more variation in size in the middle zone of this second sample than in the first sample.

> *There is so much to by with such speed to making the most if a day will ever*

Now let's look at an accountant's writing. The sample below shows a left slant with half-and-half connectedness, normal line spacing, and word spacing that is normal to slightly wide. This accountant has good planning and organizational skills, is careful, checks out the facts, and will make sure that everything is correct.

> We recently saw a
> about nasty neighbours
> this we thought we
> neighbour has a lot
> has planted a hedge

In the next sample we have a lawyer's writing – small size, a fine stroke, wide line and word spacing with simplified style. This shows a clear mind that is able to dig deep to get to the bottom of a problem. It also shows that this person prefers to work alone so that full concentration can be given to all aspects of the case. This is a very clever person who can see the whole picture

> The hearing is due to take place
> 2 pm. We have prepared the
> be grateful if you would sign

as well as having a good eye for detail. In the following sample we have a scientist's writing. Look at the size of his writing – the smaller you write, the more intense your concentration. He has very wide line spacing and his word spacing is also large. Although the writing is connected, it is quite difficult to read – let's hope he can read his own writing! He also has broad width which shows that he is willing to look at all aspects when he is at work. He likes to do a thorough job.

Force is the rate of change of momentum

For every action there is an equal and opposite

$$v^2 - u^2 = 2as \qquad v = u + at$$

The sample below shows the writing of a vet. She has a right slant and connected writing which has some flowery style in the lower zone. Here is someone who is understanding and can talk kindly to her patients. She has many ideas and will look at her various medicines before choosing the best remedy for each animal.

Mowgli was x-rayed today he was limping on his front leg. He was given some table which will hopefully make hir

Things to Do

Have you ever thought of writing with your other hand? If you are left-handed, try writing with your right hand. If you are right-handed, try writing with your left hand. If you continue to practice with your other hand, you will find that it becomes easier and your writing starts to flow. You may also find that you start to have different ideas as you write, and this will help you to develop your own creativity and imagination.

While you are growing up you will find that your writing changes. See if you can find some writing from when you first learned to use a pencil or pen. Even your drawings and paintings will change as you develop your creativity.

Start keeping a record of your writing. Perhaps you could do this at the beginning and end of each school term. Set aside your first and last pieces of homework, or maybe start writing to a friend. Keep the record of your writing in a large scrapbook and make a note of the age you are each time you write. This information will be helpful when you have grown up because you will be able to see the gradual changes in your writing as they happen – this will be the story of your life in writing.

How do you know that your writing really does reflect your good points? Writing comes from the brain, and when you write you think. Try writing a few lines about your favorite animal while talking about something else at the same time. You will find it impossible!

Do you ever go to the beach? Try writing in the sand with your toe – you will see that there is a similarity to your normal handwriting.

Start collecting the handwritten envelopes that arrive at your home. Try to find two envelopes that have been written by different people and yet which have exactly the same writing. Let me know if you succeed because I have never known two people to write in the same way!

Something else to do when you see handwritten envelopes is to guess who has written the letter before the envelope is opened. You will be amazed by how quickly you learn to recognize other people's handwriting.

If you have just moved to a new area or are away from your friends at the moment, ask the people around you what they like about you. Ask each one on his or her own, because this will make him or her give you his or her own opinion instead of agreeing with what the other people say. You can also try this with your best friend or perhaps the people in your gang. Once again, it is important to ask them individually, when no one else is around, to make sure that you hear the many positive aspects of your character. You will be surprised by the way each friend sees you differently. Write down all the nice things that each friend says about you.

A-Z of Character Traits

Accurate	Small size narrow width simplified
Active	Right slant narrow word spacing rising baseline heavy pressure
Active mind	Wavy baselines simplified irregular
Adaptable	Small size right slant mixed slant broad width light pressure
Adventurous	Large size right slant broad width heavy pressure irregular wide word spacing
Alert	Light pressure simplified irregular
Ambitious	Large size large upper zone rising baseline heavy pressure
Analytical	Upright slant wide line spacing thin stroke simplified
Artistic	Flowery irregular disconnected thick stroke

Attends to detail	Small size narrow width regular
Balanced approach to people	Medium pressure normal word spacing half-and-half connected
Bold	Marked right slant rising baseline large size irregular heavy pressure
Calm	Straight baseline regular rhythm medium pressure copybook
Careful	Small size narrow width regular connected wide word spacing
Cautious	Left slant narrow width connected wide word spacing wide line spacing small size regular
Cheerful	Rising baseline right slant broad width thick stroke flowery
Clear thinking	Wide line spacing simplified thin stroke upright slant connected normal line spacing
Compassionate	Right slant flowery medium size
Concentrates in short bursts	Narrow line spacing mixed slant light pressure
Concentrates well	Small size narrow width simplified style regular connected straight baseline heavy pressure small middle zone
Conscientious	Small middle zone narrow width regular
Consistent	Upright slant medium size narrow width normal width normal word spacing connected medium pressure copybook regular rhythm
Conventional	Medium size copybook regular

Courageous	Right slant large size rising baseline heavy pressure
Creative	Broad width narrow line spacing flowery irregular disconnected thick stroke arrhythm
Curious	Right slant broad width irregular connected
Decisive	Heavy pressure simplified upright slant
Dependable	Straight baseline upright slant medium size medium pressure regular copybook connected
Determined	Right slant left slant straight baseline connected heavy pressure regular
Easy-going	Right slant normal width medium size thick stroke medium pressure broad width rhythm flowery
Energetic	Large size large lower zone heavy pressure right slant rising baseline
Enjoys being part of a team	Upright slant medium size normal width half-and-half connected regular normal word spacing copybook
Enjoys being with people	Upright thick stroke large middle zone narrow word spacing large size
Enjoys travel	Disconnected irregular thick stroke
Enterprising	Large size right slant broad width disconnected heavy pressure rising baseline simplified irregular
Enthusiastic	Large size right slant broad width rising baseline heavy pressure flowery irregular thick stroke

Excitable	Arrhythm irregular large size
Fair	Connected straight baseline simplified upright slant
Far-sighted	Large upper zone wide line spacing right slant
Flamboyant	Large size flowery heavy pressure
Flexible	Mixed slant normal width normal word spacing irregular half-and-half connected thick stroke
Friendly	Right slant normal word spacing broad width half-and-half connected thick stroke flowery irregular large middle zone light pressure
Full of practical ideas	Mixed slant simplified half-and-half connected
Generous	Right slant broad width flowery
Gentle	Right slant medium pressure rhythm
Genuine	Broad width irregular flowery
Good all-rounder	Upright slant medium size normal width half-and-half connected
Good-humored	Broad width rising baseline flowery
Good leader	Large size normal line spacing simplified
Good listener	Right slant rhythm half-and-half connected
Good mixer	Right slant thick stroke flowery
Good organizer	Small size larger lower zone wide word spacing wide line spacing straight baseline simplified

Good planner	Connected normal line spacing wide line spacing straight baseline regular wide word spacing
Graceful	Rhythm normal word spacing light pressure
Happy	Normal width rhythm medium size
Hard-worker	Straight baseline heavy pressure thin stroke small size normal width small middle zone
Helpful	Broad width medium size straight baseline normal word spacing
Hopeful	Right slant broad width rising baseline flowery
Idealistic	Thin stroke large upper zone irregular
Imaginative	Large size broad width disconnected flowery irregular large middle zone thick stroke
Impartial	Medium size upright slant normal width
Impulsive	Broad width narrow word spacing narrow line spacing heavy pressure irregular large size right slant rising baseline thick stroke
Inclined to compromise	Upright slant normal width medium size
Independent	Large size small lower zone upright slant left slant straight baseline simplified
Individualist	Flowery irregular arrhythm mixed slant disconnected
Industrious	Thin stroke connected straight baseline heavy pressure

Informal	Right slant broad width narrow word spacing irregular
Inner harmony	Right slant normal width rhythm
Intellectual	Large upper zone small middle zone wide line spacing
Intelligent	Normal word spacing simplified normal line spacing
Inventive	Disconnected irregular broad width
Keeps distance from others	Left slant wide word spacing small size
Kind	Right slant broad width flowery narrow word spacing
Level-headed	Upright slant medium size normal width straight baseline normal line spacing regular
Likes a routine	Medium size normal width regular connected copybook
Likes lots of variety	Arrhythm mixed slant disconnected
Likes to conform	Upright slant medium size normal width copybook regular
Likes to keep options open	Wavy baseline right slant mixed slant flowery irregular arrhythm
Literary	Wide word spacing thick stroke flowery
Lively	Broad width large size right slant
Logical	Small size upright slant connected normal line spacing thin stroke simplified
Lots of interests	Broad width thick stroke mixed slant disconnected irregular arrhythm

Loves travel	Right slant broad width disconnected
Loving	Broad width normal word spacing rhythm
Mature	Normal width normal word spacing rhythm simplified
Mentally agile	Light pressure disconnected simplified
Modest	Left slant small size small middle zone
Musical	Broad width wide word spacing rhythm
Needs time to be alone	Left slant wide word spacing small size
Objective in outlook	Small size upright slant half-and-half connected normal word spacing straight baseline simplified normal width
Observant	Small size simplified thin stroke
Open-minded	Right slant large size broad width normal line spacing
Optimistic	Large size right slant broad width rising baseline irregular
Orderly	Narrow width wide line spacing regular straight baseline simplified wide word spacing
Organizing ability	Large lower zone wide word spacing normal line spacing
Outgoing	Right slant broad width narrow word spacing thick stroke
Patient	Rhythm medium size medium pressure
Perfectionist	Narrow width regular small size
Persevering	Rising baseline heavy pressure regular

Persistent	Narrow width connected heavy pressure regular
Persuasive	Right slant broad width heavy pressure irregular
Possesses integrity	Normal width normal line spacing straight baseline simplified
Practical	Medium size small lower zone left slant simplified broad width half-and-half connected normal line spacing irregular
Prefers action to reflection	Large size heavy pressure rising baseline
Prefers one-to-one contact	Left slant wide word spacing thin stroke small middle zone
Punctual	Regular rhythm
Quick-thinking	Mixed slant simplified half-and-half connected
Quiet	Left slant small size small middle zone
Rational	Upright slant narrow word spacing simplified half-and-half connected
Ready for new situations	Right slant large size broad width thick stroke irregular
Realistic	Small size small upper zone large middle zone thick stroke simplified upright slant normal width normal line spacing
Receptive to new ideas	Right slant broad width rising baseline disconnected
Reliable	Small size upright slant straight baseline heavy pressure regular
Scientific	Small size narrow width connected simplified

Secretive	Left slant narrow width wide word spacing
Self-assured	Wide line spacing rhythm upright slant thick stroke
Self-confident	Large size broad width normal word spacing normal line spacing
Self-contained	Thin stroke simplified rhythm small size
Self-controlled	Small size upright slant left slant straight baseline simplified
Self-disciplined	Narrow width regular heavy pressure simplified connected
Self-reliant	Small upper zone upright slant simplified
Self-sufficient	Small size simplified upright slant
Sense of humor	Broad width thick stroke flowery irregular
Sense of justice	Upright slant straight baseline connected simplified
Sense of proportion	Upright slant medium size normal width
Sensible	Rhythm half-and-half connected upright slant normal width
Sensitive	Right slant light pressure thin stroke irregular arrhythm disconnected
Sentimental	Flowery right slant large size
Shy	Left slant narrow width wide word spacing light pressure thin pen
Single-minded	Narrow width regular left slant connected heavy pressure
Sociable	Right slant large size small upper zone small lower zone broad width flowery

Spontaneous	Right slant large size broad width narrow line spacing irregular disconnected arrhythm large middle zone
Stable	Upright slant normal width straight baseline medium pressure copybook regular
Steady worker	Medium size connected medium or heavy pressure straight baseline regular rhythm
Straightforward	Straight baseline rhythm simplified
Sympathetic	Right slant broad width flowery
Systematic	Narrow width connected simplified regular
Talkative	Large size narrow word spacing right slant flowery thick stroke connected
Tenacious	Heavy pressure connected small size regular
Thinks deeply	Thin stroke connected large lower zone heavy pressure
Thorough	Wide line spacing connected heavy pressure
Thrifty	Small size narrow width thin stroke
Tolerant	Normal line spacing rhythm broad width
Trusting	Narrow word spacing thick stroke medium size
Trustworthy	Straight baseline simplified flowery
Varied interests	Broad width disconnected thick stroke flowery irregular

Versatile	Mixed slant broad width wavy baseline disconnected irregular
Vivacious	Broad width rising baseline thick stroke irregular
Well-meaning	Narrow word spacing narrow line spacing rhythm

Answers

Chapter 2   A lady aged 49.

Chapter 7   **Quiz** – Thick stroke.
                       Puzzle – Yes, thick stroke, right slant and irregular.

Chapter 8   **Quiz** – No.
                       Puzzle – No, not with such large size!
                       Eager Beaver – "U" is the letter "n" upside down.

Chapter 9   **Quiz** – Yes. The slant is always to the left. If you think
                       it is different, perhaps you have been looking at the
                       angle of the slant which does change.
                       Puzzle – Yes. The third movement could be connected.

Chapter 10   **Quiz** – Connected.
                       Puzzle – No, it is arrhythmic, so the writer likes
                       variety.

Chapter 11   **Quiz** – The letter "f".
                       Puzzle – Yes – small size, connected, narrow.

Chapter 12   **Quiz** – It is important to have several samples of writing because baselines show our feelings. We may be sad or tired one day and our baselines will fall, but the next day we are happy and so the baselines rise.
Puzzle – Yes – there is heavy pressure, connected writing and wide word spacing.

Chapter 13   **Quiz** – Word spacing is wide.
Puzzle – Yes, he has legible writing, wide word spacing and dovetailing lines.
Eager Beaver – Yes, once more in line eight where the "f" in "midfield" does not touch the "t" in "Manchester" on the line below.

Chapter 14   **Quiz** – It is quicker to write with irregular writing. Try it and see for yourself.
Puzzle – A person with irregular writing will be more flexible. If you have regular writing you will want to know what you are doing and then get on with it. You will not like to keep having your plans changed.
Puzzle – The writer prefers doing lots of different activities for a short time as he has irregular writing, broad width and mixed slant.

Chapter 15   **Quiz** – In fact, there are two other movements – one is spacing which you have already read about and the other is pressure which we shall look at in the next chapter.
Puzzle – Yes, the writing is fairly regular, connected and small size.

Chapter 16   **Quiz** – Many thousands of copies of this book have been printed, so it is impossible to enclose original pieces of writing in each copy.
Puzzle – Someone with light pressure gets tired more quickly than someone with heavy pressure.

Two samples – There is one in the History and Origins section and one in the puzzle in the Baselines chapter.

Chapter 17   **Quiz** – No. No one can write in the exact way he or she was taught because we are all unique. Although two pieces of writing may look alike, there will be differences between them.

Puzzle – No, because it is irregular, disconnected and arrhythmic.

Now that you have finished this book, you may be interested in learning about graphology in more depth. Send for information on courses. You can learn either on your own with a teach yourself method, or by correspondence with your own tutor. Write to Jacqui Tew at 60 Netherby Park, Weybridge, Surrey KT13 0AQ, England.